The Laser Campaign Manual

Revised April 2003

www.fernhurstbooks.co.uk

The Laser
Campaign
Manual

Ben Ainslie

fernhurst
B O O K S

Text and photos © Fernhurst Books 2003
Contents of CD © Fernhurst Books 2003

First published 2002 by
Fernhurst Books,
Duke's Path, High Street, Arundel,
West Sussex, BN18 9AJ, United Kingdom.

British Library Cataloguing in Publication Data.
A catalogue record for this book is available
from the British Library.

ISBN 1 898660 90 5

Printed in China through World Print.

Photography by Dave Giles and Peter Bentley,
represented by PPL Photo Agency Ltd
Tel: +44 (0)1243 555561.
E.mail: ppl@mistral.co.uk
Website: www.pplmedia.com

Ben Ainslie CD produced by PPL Multimedia.
Tel: + 44(0)1243 555561.
E.mail: ppl@mistral.co.uk
Website: www.pplmedia.com
Video: Dave Giles/PPL
Programming: Neill Blume/PPL

Photographs of the Laser Worlds
by Michael Austen.

The photos of the new control systems were
provided by Mark Littlejohn, full-time Olympic
Laser and Europe coach and a top Laser and
Laser Master sailor.
Contact him on his email:
littlejohn_mark@hotmail.com

The author and publisher would like to thank
the Royal Lymington Yacht Club for their kind
hospitality during the photography sessions.

Artwork by Creative Byte.

Cover design by Simon Balley.
Edited by Tim Davison and Chloe Davison.

Contents

Introduction

The Laser 7
Goal Setting 7
Money 8
Sponsorship 8
Time 8
Learning 9

Part 1 Getting the boat right

Checking the hull 10
Putting the boat together 11
The rudder and tiller 11
Toestrap and ratchet block 13
Hatches 13
Control lines 14
Cunningham 14
Boom vang 15
Outhaul 16
Mainsheet 17
Centreboard 17
Telltales 19
Mast 19
Fittings 19
Cleats 19

Part 2 Speed around the course

Starting 20
Practising starting 21
Beating in medium winds 22
Beating in light airs 25
Beating in strong winds 28
Footing and pointing 31
Tacking 32
Tacking in light winds 34
Tacking in strong winds 36
Rounding the windward mark 38
Reaching in medium winds 40
Reaching in light airs 44
Reaching in strong winds 46
Gybing in medium winds 48
Roll gybing in light airs 52
Gybing in strong winds 53
Running in medium winds 54
Running in light airs 58
Running in strong winds 62
Approaching the leeward mark 66
720 degree turns 68
Capsizing 70

Part 3 Let's get personal

Diet 71

Training 71

Racing 71

Fitness 73

Sailing fitness 73

Land training 73

Aerobic fitness 73

Weight training 74

Sports specific exercises 74

Training 77

On your own 77

Boat handling 77

Something different 77

Training partner 77

Coaching 78

Training methods 78

Clothing 80

Hiking shorts 80

Boots 80

Part 4 How to win a championship

Countdown to a particular event 81

Logistics 81

The venue 82

Weaknesses 82

Fitness 82

Peaking 82

Racing to win 84

Psychology 84

A typical race day 86

Exercising in the boat 88

The race 89

Pre-start 89

Starting 89

Accelerating off the line 90

The first 100m 90

Which way up the first beat? 90

Windward mark 91

Reaching 92

Running 92

Leeward gates and gybe marks 93

Consolidation 94

About the CD 96

Introduction

Dinghy sailing started for me when, as a ten year old, I woke up one Christmas morning to find an Optimist dinghy beside my bed. I guess I have been sailing mad ever since.

Growing up by the water near Falmouth meant that I could sail as much as I wanted and I was fortunate that there was a great sailing club nearby in Restronguet. One of the local sailing heroes, Phil Slater, started weekend coaching and it wasn't long before he had made us the top Optimist club in the country. The racing was ultra-competitive and half the time we would charge around thinking we were Chris Dickson or Russell Coutts; it was a lot of fun and it was great preparation for the future. I did well in the Optimist, achieving some good results nationally but was never able to perform that well internationally or find any consistency in my sailing.

I remember one race in particular. I had been winning but got some windshifts wrong and lost two places, to my arch-rivals David Lenz and Darren Williams. I slumped down in the boat thinking how unfair life was and all the rest of it, without realising that my Dad was right behind me watching. That night my Dad and I sat down and talked it through, deciding that if I wanted to take the sport seriously and be successful then I had to be prepared to go for it and give it 100%. My parents have always been a great support and every now and then you need someone to point you in the right direction. From that point on I was totally committed to sailing and knew there was nothing else I wanted to do. It was also around that time that I matured enough to realise I had to think for myself regarding my sailing and performance, and it was due to this that I started making big improvements.

The Laser

The Laser may appear to be a very simple boat, which I suppose in some ways it is. But the strict one design aspect means that it is very small differences in technique, boat set-up and psychology which make the difference.

What has always attracted me to single-handed sailing is the freedom. There is no crew to argue with, it's just you, the boat and the rest of the fleet. There is no one to blame or praise and the performance on the water is down to your efforts; you alone make the difference.

It does take a certain amount of self-discipline and determination to sail and race single-handed. The usual scenario is when you turn up to the club on a frosty winter's morning to find most people have decided they would be better off staying in bed. Do you head off to your local for a pint or take the opportunity to spend some more hours on the water training and make a gain?

One of the great things about the Laser is that whatever your situation, whether it be club sailor or Olympic hopeful, you will always find competition at your level to race against. You often find there is a great camaraderie between people especially between races and ashore.

Goal setting

One of the most important things to decide from the outset is what you want to achieve. It doesn't matter whether your goal is to win the club championship or an Olympic gold - you need an aim and something to work towards.

It is important to be realistic with your goals and try to take things step-by-step. Since I was ten I dreamed of winning a gold medal and when

I became a Laser sailor that dream became more of a reality, but there was still an Everest between me and that goal. I was sixteen and remember sitting with my Dad trying to work out how I was going to get there, but it soon became obvious that I had to try and become the best youth sailor in Britain. The next step was to go for being the best in Britain and then the world. If your goals are set too high or are at best a 'long shot', then you run the risk of always falling short and after time this can be very disappointing and a real de-motivator. Similarly, if you under-estimate your ability you will not push yourself to the limits of your capability.

If the Olympics are your objective it is important to realise that a four-year goal is a long way off. Yes, it is important to have a long-term aim but it is also important to look at the short term and set goals year by year. That way you are able to re-evaluate your performance almost constantly and this will no doubt affect your goal setting and your rate of improvement.

Money

The Laser is fortunately a relatively cheap boat and the one-design aspect also means that you don't need to break the bank designing sails or foils. Also, the large number of national and international events means that you don't always need to travel abroad to find top competition.

If you want to race internationally then money is probably more of an issue. Find out if your National Authority has any grants available and how to qualify for them, which may also have an immediate effect on your goal setting.

As a youth sailor you are probably heavily dependant on your parents. Make sure they know what you are trying to achieve and why you need help. Then they will understand that it is a worthwhile cause and will hopefully be more supportive. Also try to make the most of any local or national youth training schemes, because this is the best way to access top coaching.

Be careful not to stretch your resources too far.

It can be a great strain to do something that you can't really afford and your mind will probably wander from what should be its real focus, the sailing.

Sponsorship

Sailing has always had a rather curious sporting profile ranging from the America's Cup, via Olympic sailing, to racing around the world and because of this diversification there has been no concerted effort to make the sport marketable.

Fortunately Laser sailing is an Olympic sport and so comes under the banner of the Olympic movement, which as a separate entity works hard to retain and promote the view that the Olympics is the stuff of legends and the ultimate sporting achievement.

While you may not be searching for sponsorship for an Olympic campaign, the fact that Laser sailing is an Olympic sport certainly adds credibility to any sponsorship proposal. However, realistically, unless you have a very high profile financial sponsorship is hard to come by. It is not impossible, but the fact that you have some good results is often not enough. You need to be able to offer some returns either in the way of media coverage, corporate sailing days or something along those lines.

The best way to find sponsors is through connections. Check all your family and friends. They may know someone who is a marketing manager; at least then you have an introduction. Sometimes working with other sailors to form a team can open more doors, as many companies seem to have a policy of only sponsoring teams.

It is also possible to try and pick up sponsorship in kind. You could go to your local Laser supplier and ask for a discount on kit. Also a clothing sponsor can save you money, and at least you will look the part!

Time

There really is no substitute for time on the water. Full-time sailors spend as much as 25 hours a week training on the water, and it shows.

Obviously if you are trying to hold down a full time job or have a family you will not be able to put in that much commitment but again it depends on what you want to achieve and being realistic about your situation. One way to make more time is obviously to try and manage your time better, but also if you can get a good routine going that always seems to save time. If you have to decide between keeping to your fitness routine and time on the water, in almost all circumstances I would say your time would be far better spent on the water. It's more fun as well.

It can take a long time to get where you want. I started Radial sailing at 15 and moved into the full rig at 17. It wasn't until I was 21 that I won my first senior world title so that's four years of non-stop full-time racing and training in the standard Laser. In the end all of us have only so much time sailing so the key to it all is - enjoy it.

Learning

I don't think I have ever gone on the water and not learned something. Ultimately it is essential to increase your performance. You go out on the water, make a mistake, learn from it and try not to make the same mistake again. Obviously it is not as simple as that, but a top Laser sailor must always be on the lookout for ways to improve, be it through fitness, technique, boat set-up or psychology. The moment when you sit back and think you have made it to the top is probably the time when you will get a nasty reminder that the rest of the fleet is still improving and will probably leave you behind.

Reading sailing books and watching sailing videos are also great ways to feed your mind and get you thinking about how to improve. I love watching America's Cup racing. Although it may not be applicable to Laser sailing it still gets me thinking about the sport, while being a lot of fun. I'm not sure if my parents would agree on that, but the tape has nearly worn out.

Part 1
Getting the boat right

One of the great advantages of Laser sailing is being able to go anywhere, borrow a boat and know that it will be as good, or nearly as good, as your boat at home.

It is a relatively simple boat to put together and rig but there are still some tricks to setting up the boat properly and making life easier for yourself.

CHECKING THE HULL

When you collect your boat, be it new or used, check it over – this can save a lot of time. New boats vary very little (the one-design tolerances are tight) but older boats may have gained weight or had some disaster in their past which has affected the key measurements. You certainly don't want a boat that is heavy, for obvious reasons. It is important on older boats to check the mast rake. You don't want the mast raked a long way back, because you won't be able to get enough leech tension on the mainsail,

causing the leech to flap even in moderate winds. You will also find that you suffer more from weather helm. Similarly you do not want the mast raked too far forwards as this creates more mast bend, giving large diagonal creases from the mast join to the clew. What you are really looking for is something in the middle. To check, put the bottom mast in the boat and 'rake' it back. Hook the end of a tape measure to the top/back of the mast and measure to the middle of the round of the transom. 148 inches is raked back, 152 inches is raked forward. If in doubt, forward is better because it's quick downwind and you get good leech tension upwind.

Next, measure from the top of the bottom mast to each gunwale to make sure the rig is vertical.

Check all the spars for bends, etc. Again, you will not need to worry if you are buying new. I prefer a bottom mast that is bendy, so given the choice would go for one with minimum weight or which appears to have a thin wall.

Measure the rake with a tape measure from the top of the bottom mast to the middle of the transom's round.

Measure like this to each gunwale:
is the mast vertical?

Check that the rudder and centreboard
are in line.

Check the bottom of the boat for scratches and also for any unevenness in the hull - using a flat piece of wood will highlight this. The nature of the construction (the Laser is still hand laid-up) means there will nearly always be some unevenness but, clearly, don't pick one that is worse than the others! The Laser rules forbid you from long board sanding your boat so you need to have it right from the beginning. I don't 'prepare' the hull or foils in any way.

Make sure your trolley is well padded and that you have some decent covers because manoeuvring ashore is the easiest way to damage your boat.

Turn the boat upside-down with the centreboard in its case and the rudder attached. You will now be able to check if both the centreboard and rudder are straight and line up. You may need to adjust the rudder gudgeons if the rudder is off-line.

PUTTING THE BOAT TOGETHER

I'm not going to go through rigging the boat - everyone knows how to do that. Let's just have a look at a few things you may not have thought of.

The rudder and tiller

Make sure the rudder can go down as far as the rules allow - the trailing edge must be in line with the rudder stock.

Replace the bolt with a bigger one, and tighten it so the blade is locked down; in essence you now have a fixed rudder. When you launch or come ashore, lift off the rudder and tiller as one unit and put it under the traveller.

There is now no need for a purchase on the downhaul 'within' the rudder head, but I do have one near the cleat.

Trailing edge in line with stock.

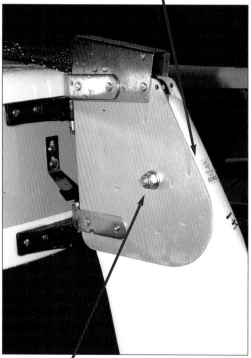

Bigger bolts.

The main features you are looking for in a tiller are that it is strong, fits well in your rudder stock, is neither too low nor too high above the traveller cleat and is light. If the tiller sits too high then you will struggle to get enough traveller tension, if it is too low then it will bang on the cleat.

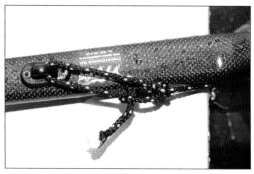

My rudder purchase is near the cleat.

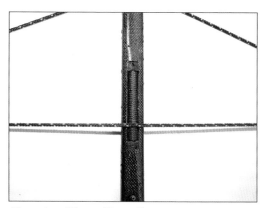

My carbon tiller, with a roller.

There are quite a few good manufacturers of carbon tillers - Marstrand from Sweden, MB Yachting from New Zealand, C2 Composites, Rooster Sailing and Laser Direct based in England. I used the NZ tiller because it was the best. I believe Laser Direct have developed a low profile carbon tiller which sounds good.

This is the length of the tiller extension that I use.

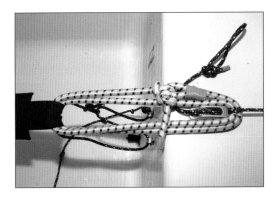

The tiller extension needs to be the right length for you. To find out what suits you best go out with an old extension which is too long and slowly cut it down until it feels right. You can then measure that one against your carbon extension to get it the right length. The photo on page 12 shows the length of my tiller extension.

Toestrap and ratchet block

My ideal toestrap is well-padded and short, to give space for the adjuster rope. Remember, you adjust it after the windward mark and before the leeward mark.

Move the friction pad forward a bit, to keep the centreboard down.

Spending a bit more on a decent ratchet block is definitely worth it. You will find it causes a lot less wear on the mainsheet and is also smoother. Ronstan, Harken or Fredriksen make good blocks.

Hatches

I have never bothered with hatches in my boat as they always seem to leak. If you can hear bits of fibreglass rattling inside your boat, then it might be an idea to put a hatch in by the centreboard case; this way you will be able to get rid of the loose glass and save some weight.

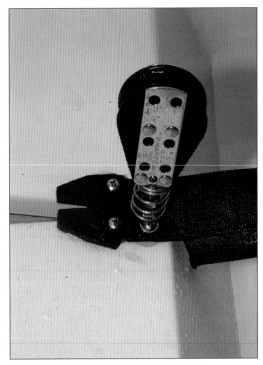

Move the friction pad forward to keep the centreboard down.

CONTROL LINES

I am showing the new control lines here, but my views on them are developing. Click the publisher's website for my latest thoughts. Much of this material was kindly provided by Mark Littlejohn, who led the development team.

Basically, from 1 October 2001 you can go for a retrofitted rigging package incorporating blocks to bring both the cunningham and outhaul controls to the centre of the deck to a new double camcleat arrangement. There is also an entirely new swivel vang (kicker) system. These new systems are simple to rig, provide more precise control and are easily adjusted from the hiking position permitting, for the first time in the Laser, adjustments to be made on any point of sailing. The new rule is based on a controlled number of purchases in each system. The new options can be cherry-picked to suit individual requirements and blocks can be added to the old systems in place of the rope knots and loops to provide a low-cost upgrade.

The cunningham

This is similar to the old system, but with two pieces of rope, and blocks. The photos show how it's rigged. The new blocks dramatically reduce friction and increase the range of control available. With less friction, the cunningham is more easily applied while sailing upwind, which was previously very difficult to achieve, particularly for the smaller sailor in strong winds. Lean back, and pull with straight arms. When sailing downwind the cunningham eases out more efficiently when released.

Have the ropes on either side of the boom, except in very strong winds or with an old sail when you may need the whole system on one side so you can pull the grommet right down.

Many sailors who use a multi-purchase system at the moment could upgrade to the new purchase system and gain greatly reduced friction, or use a lower purchase ratio giving faster control response.

Boom vang (kicking strap)

The new vang system will transform downwind sailing. A swivelling cleat makes adjusting the

vang tension a joy from all positions in the boat, either when hiking out or sitting in. The new vang can be let off and pulled on in all downwind conditions, which was previously very difficult. For example, when bearing away from a reach to a run, the vang tension can easily be adjusted. Likewise, when sailing on a reach it's a simple matter of pulling on more vang if you need to sail higher – again, this was previously impossible in medium to strong winds. But take care, with the power available in the new system it's now very easy to over-apply the vang!

Mark the vang rope (in ink) at various places, building up a set of 'fast marks' for all points of sailing. This makes changing the tension quicker and more accurate.

Take a long tail from the vang handle to the centreboard, so you can always reach the rope.

The vang's pin still has a tendency to fall out of the boom, so tie a piece of elastic around the boom to hold it in.

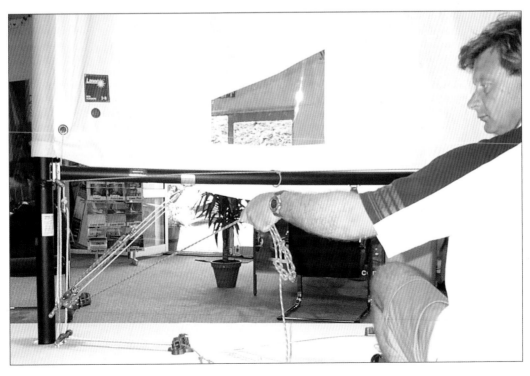

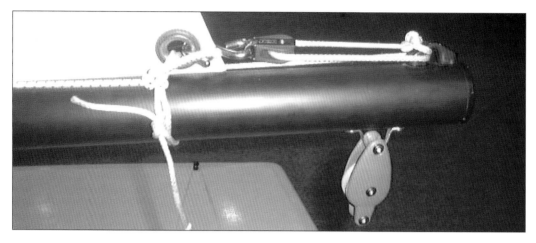

The outhaul

The outhaul stays on the boom permanently.

At the boom end the arrangement is similar to the old one, but the pulley and hook are a great improvement. The rope is deadeyed as normal, and the tie-down is the same: push the clew one side of the boom, wrap the rope around twice and tie a reef knot.

Use a piece of elastic to pull the clew towards the mast. Tie the other end to the old boom cleat (as shown here) or to the moving block.

The red rope gives another 2:1. It is tied to the cleat, goes through a 'floating' block and then passes through a permanently-attached block at the gooseneck. Finally, it goes through a block at the foot of the mast, and to the new cleat.

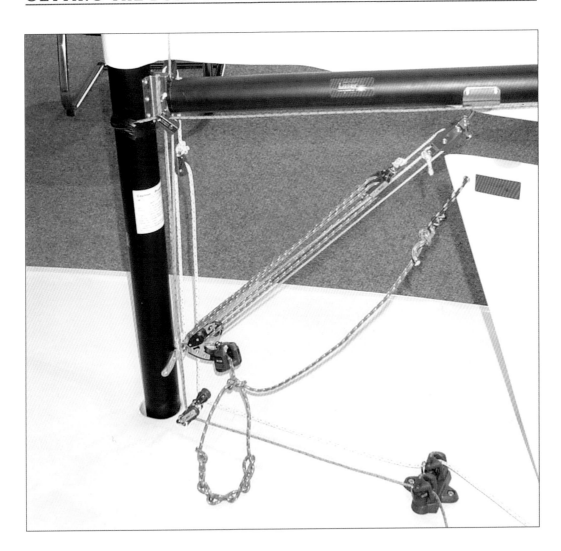

A refinement is to tie a loop in the red rope around the boom, to stop the whole thing drooping (see page 15).

You will get the most benefit when sailing downwind; previously you couldn't adjust the outhaul but now you can. Also, life will be easier at the windward and leeward marks.

Small adjustments to the outhaul have a significant effect on speed. Be careful not to let off too much downwind – use a maximum mark.

Mainsheet

Use 14 m of 5.8 or 7 mm Polilite.

Centreboard

You need 6 - 8 mm elastic to hold up the centreboard. Tie a bowline around the bow fitting and fix a clip at the other end, which should hook onto a loop coming from the front of the centreboard. Don't have the elastic too tight, or it pulls up the centreboard. To make a handle on the centreboard drill two holes about 4 inches apart on the top of the centreboard and use rope to make a handle.

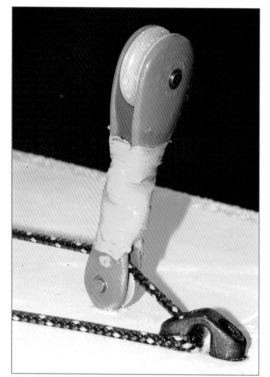

Above: Tape the traveller blocks or they will kink.

Above right: Seal around the bailer screw.

Right: My Windex, taped onto the bow eye.

Make one fold near the head, then roll the sail like this.

Telltales

Telltales are a vital guide to how the sail is being trimmed and set up. I use one telltale at the top of the sail in line with the top batten, and another between the window and the luff of the sail. The top telltale helps when adjusting the vang and trimming the sail downwind. If it is not flying (and is showing the sail is under-trimmed) while the bottom telltale is flying then this indicates that the vang is too loose. If the top telltale flies and the bottom of the sail looks under-trimmed then the vang is too tight. The bottom telltale is also a good indicator both upwind and while reaching, in conjunction with the wind indicator.

Mast

If the bottom mast is bent you have no option but to buy a new one.

Straighten the topmast as in the photo. When putting the mast together, use tape to give the plugs a tight fit into the bottom mast. This will stop the mast twisting out of line and prevent movement inside the mast.

Fittings

Make sure that you have plenty of sealant under all your fittings. It is amazing how the water manages to find its way in. Also make sure all of the fittings are screwed in tightly as this may have been overlooked.

Cleats

If you are going to use cleats make sure they are as small as possible (either Ronstan or Harken mini-cleats) and as far forward as possible, so as not to restrict your legs while hiking or your backside while sitting in.

Part 2
Speed around
the course

STARTING

Your objective is to stay in position on the line, keeping the boat into the wind. Make sure the vang is off because that makes

manoeuvring easier.

You will need to use the tiller to stay head to wind but it is illegal to scull. A good indication of when you are about to break the rule is if the

boat starts to go forwards. This is clearly prohibited under Rule 42.

Sometimes you will need to tack and tack back to hold your position. Push the boom out as you turn, to stop you moving forward over the line.

When you're ready to go, pull on the vang. Let out the sheet and use the tiller to steer the boat around to a close reaching angle. With five seconds to go, hike the boat flat and come onto the wind gradually, sheeting in. Go, go, go!

CD Now view the Starting video on the CD

PRACTISING STARTING

In a race you'll need to keep station in a gap on the startline or by the committee boat. To practise, use the tiller to hold your boat head to wind and in position. Be aware that it is illegal to scull so don't allow your tiller to cross the boat's centreline continually. Also try tacking back and forth to hold the boat in the same position.

Sometimes you need to reverse out of a poor spot on the line and go somewhere else, so practise sailing backwards. Obviously, 30 seconds to go is too late to change position but two minutes to go is ok.

Starting: control, tack, accelerate.

BEATING IN MEDIUM WINDS

In medium airs the difference between fast and slow is very little, especially on flat water. In waves there can be more of a speed difference as technique plays a part. In medium winds the top sailors are often the ones who can keep good speed while looking around the fleet and the course to decide on their tactics and strategy. When the fleet is going roughly the same speed it is where you put your boat that will determine the finishing result. In short, sail fast and keep your head out of the boat.

To get through a chop it's important to have a bit of power in the sail so don't pull on too much outhaul or vang. As you become overpowered start tightening the vang, outhaul and then cunningham until the boat feels better balanced.

Toestrap

It's important to keep your toestrap adjusted to the right length or your body movements won't translate into speed. (Too loose and you won't put enough force through the boat.) A good setting is equal pressure on your calves and the backs of your thighs.

Steering

If the water is flat then it is fastest to let the boat almost sail itself, keeping the boat balance and steering even and smooth. In waves it's important to keep looking ahead: it you see a bad set of waves, bear away a bit to get around them.

Body movement and steering

Lean back hard coming into the wave and steer up (ie lift up and lean back just before the wave). This helps push the boat up the wave, gaining height and speed.

As you come over the wave bear away slightly and move your body forwards to help the boat go down the back of the wave.

Use plenty of steering to guide the boat through the waves.

Heel

Heel slightly to leeward. If you see a big wave coming heel more so the water slides off the boat rather than coming into the cockpit.

Wave technique

Cunningham

Just tight enough to bring the creases out of the sail.

Outhaul

Important! Sail quite full to get through the waves but not so full that there's too much drag or you are overpowered.

Mainsheet

Always two-blocked unless you have to bear away for a bad set of waves.

Vang

Quite loose. When you ease the sheet it wants to give the sail more shape. (When two-blocked, there's still tension in the vang.)

Sit

Move your weight forwards and backwards constantly. Slide your backside as well as leaning backwards and forewards.

If you get a good wave underneath you, move your weight forward and ride down it nicely. Other times in a bad bit of chop, work your body weight backwards.

Centreboard

Right down. To stop it coming up you should have moved the friction pad forward and not have the elastic too tight (which pulls the centreboard up). If it does come up, kick it down with your front foot.

Gusts

Pull on some vang and be prepared to hike harder!

Lulls

Ease the vang and move your body weight forwards.

Common mistakes

Most people don't ease the sheet if they hit a wave and slow down; don't look ahead at the waves that are coming; don't move their body weight enough.

Beating in light airs.

BEATING IN LIGHT AIRS

Aims

The key to light air sailing is to keep the boat
moving. You need to get the foils working which
will then give you lift. Once you have the boat
up to speed you can then look for height while
being very careful not to stall the boat. One of
the best light wind sailors is Paul Goodison; he
is able to keep his boat moving very quickly
through the water, constantly altering course
very subtly, gaining height to windward when
he can and then diving for speed when he feels
the boat is beginning to stall. Body weight is
important in light airs with lighter sailors
commonly being able to sail at a closer angle
to the wind without stalling the boat than their
heavier counterparts. Heavier sailors need to
keep the boat moving even if it means losing
a few degrees in height to the lighter sailors,
as once you have stalled the boat you lose a lot
of ground trying to get it back up to speed.

Outhaul

The furthest distance between the boom and
sail is the same as the distance from your
watch to your fingertips. This gives some
power in the sail but it's not too full so you
still have pointing ability.

Cunningham

Set so the creases are only just showing.

Vang

A tiny bit more than block-to-block. When you
ease the sheet the sail shouldn't go up in the
air too much.

If the breeze builds you will need to pull on the
Cunningham so that the creases are not as
prominent and also the outhaul should be pulled
to stop the sail becoming too deep in the lower
half. The outhaul may also need tightening if the

wind is very light (under 4 knots) and the water is flat, as a sail which is too deep will cause what wind there is to stall over the sail.

Trim

The best trim for light airs is dead flat or a slight heel to leeward. On flat water keeping the boat flat will give you the most power from the rig and foils. But if the wind is gusty it may be better to keep a slight leeward heel, because in a sudden lull the boat will then go flat rather than heel to windward which is slow as it induces lee helm.

In waves or a chop the best trim is with a slight leeward heel. In waves the boat will be knocked around and will be generally less steady. Having a leeward heel will enable you to prevent the windward heel but also help you to steer around waves and also accelerate if the boat hits a bad wave.

Sit

As far forward as possible (front leg in front of the mainsheet). In a light spot move your weight in to keep the boat flat. Keep your feet in a position where you can move around easily.

Body movement and steering

In flat water it is really a case of being as subtle as possible with your body movements and steering. Try to let the boat sail itself once you have pointed it in the right direction. Too much helm and body movement will just increase drag beneath the boat and disturb the airflow over the sails.

If the water is choppy then try to steer the boat around the waves, concentrating on keeping the boatspeed and not slamming into any big waves. Lean your upper body both outwards and backwards as you come to the face of a wave to try and squeeze the boat through the wave like you would in strong winds. If you find the boat has stalled then this is where your slight leeward heel comes into play. Bear away slightly (around five degrees) easing the sail to suit while at the same time bringing the boat flat which will bring it back up to speed as quickly as possible.

I prefer to steer with the tiller extension behind me as I find it easier to be precise and also it is easier to coordinate the upper body movement with the steering. You may get a few funny looks by sailing like this but be prepared to try it if it has the potential to make you faster..

Sheet

Keep it loose. In the light spots ease it out, bear away and keep the boat moving. As the breeze comes on slowly sheet on until you're block-to-block, take the speed and convert it to height. In five knots of wind you should be block-to-block.

Toestraps

As tight as possible.

Centreboard

Right down.

Common mistakes

Not moving your body weight enough to keep the boat heeled to leeward. (That way, when a lull comes the boat doesn't roll on top of you, generating lee helm.)

Sheeting on too hard.

BEATING IN STRONG WINDS

Aims

Again speed is vital to doing well upwind in strong winds. There is a common belief which I was often told when I started sailing Lasers that in a breeze you just pull the mainsail in all the way and then pinch into the wind until the boat comes flat. Don't fall for this like I did, this is probably the worst way to sail into a strong breeze. As in light winds, the faster you can get the boat going the more lift you will gain from the foils. If you try and pinch the boat you will just end up going slower and slipping sideways; hit one bad wave and you will virtually stop. Again being able to keep your head out of the boat is vital in strong winds. So often you see really fast heavy air sailors blasting off to a corner, so focused on going fast that they completely forget about the layline or some other minor tactical aspect! Having sailed over most of the fleet since the start they then wonder why there is no one left to completely demoralise, until they eventually look over their shoulder to find the rest of the fleet rounding the windward mark miles away. You have to be as smart in 30 knots as you do in 5 knots.

Sail set up

In anything over 15 knots you should be looking to de-power the rig as well as still having enough power to get the boat through the waves. If you are looking to really de-power then the cunningham needs to be as hard on as possible so that the eye on the sail is almost touching the boom; this will help to open the leech at the top of the sail. The vang should be very tight (so that when the mainsheet is eased it leaves the deck at near enough a 30 degree angle) and this will flatten the sail and also make sheeting easier and more effective.

Body movement and hiking positions

The most important thing to remember is to try and keep your upper body flat. It is very easy to become slightly slouched, when the flatter your upper body is the more righting moment you will produce.

As you approach the wave steer the boat up the face to meet the tip of the wave. Once you are over the top of the wave bear away slightly to keep the boat moving. If you don't steer into the wave you will constantly be knocked sideways and will lose a lot of height.

The size of the waves really determines the speed at which the body movements occur. In a short chop you have to hike hard to keep the boat moving. Sheet the mainsail and move the tiller to really try to push the boat through the waves.

In larger waves the movements are much slower as it takes more time to sail over the waves and this makes the whole process much smoother. As you sail up the front of the wave it is particularly important to try and gain height from the acceleration. So as you come up to the wave lean back hard and steer up, really trying to squeeze the boat up the face of the wave.

As you get yourself back in the right position for the next wave move your upper body forwards so that you have more movement available as you move your body backwards coming into the next wave.

This is my hiking style - I don't believe in straight legs!

As you make these movements forwards and backwards it is important to switch the weight on your legs. As you lean forwards the weight should be on your front leg and then switch the weight onto your back leg for the lean backwards into the wave. Switching the weight on your legs has two main purposes. Firstly it enables better flow of blood through your legs as ultimately each leg gets a short moment of relief and so slows the rate of fatigue, so that you can hike harder for longer. The other purpose is that transferring all the weight onto your back leg as you lean back into a wave is a better way of transferring that force through the boat and to push up the face of the wave.

Toestrap

The way your toestrap is set is very important if you want to have a comfortable and effective hiking position. There are really two theories to toestrap length. One is to have it as tight as possible, to the extent that you are literally hiking off your toes. This technique was first used by Kiwi sailors in the mid '90's with the benefits being that you are really locked onto the side of the boat and consequently any body movements made have a higher kinetic force through the boat. Having a tighter strap also helps to keep your backside out of the water and your upper body at a flatter angle which results in more leverage. There is one other practical benefit which is that you rarely need to adjust your toestrap during a race, saving you time. If you are going to use this technique it is very important that you slowly alter your sailing style. There have been many sailors who have switched to this style and severely bruised and strained their ankles due to the extra strain around their feet.

Use lots of tiller movement to go over a wave.

I have never been able to use a tight toestrap as I find it uncomfortable and ineffective. Instead I just adjust my toestrap length to what is comfortable and most effective for a fast hiking style. The easiest way to get the right setting is to adjust the toestrap on the water. What you are looking for is an equal amount of pressure on your calf and hamstring muscles. If the strap is too loose you will end up with your knees in the air and if it is too tight you will find too much pressure on your ankles. Sail upwind trying slight adjustments until you feel good in the boat. Maximum toestrap length is something which will always need adjusting as your weight, height and sailing style alter.

As the wind dies and your body weight needs to come inboard it is vital to adjust the strap so that you remain locked into the boat, otherwise your body movements will not be as effective. If the wind is very gusty it can be hard to keep the strap at the right length. A way around this is to use very thick elastic between the end of the strap and the traveller cleat. If the elastic is properly adjusted it should be able to counter your weight even when you are not fully hiking and keep you locked into the boat.

Cunningham

Lots. It's impossible to have it too tight! I rig the cunningham on each side of the boom. In heavy air pull it down until the grommet touches the top of the boom.

Outhaul

Tight, but still keep some shape in the sail. There will always be a gap between the foot and the boom.

Body movement

Hike out hard!

Steering

If you see a bad set of waves coming, ease sheet and sail fast through them rather than trying to pinch. Use the waves - scoot higher up the wave. Use lots of tiller movement.

Vang

Very tight. It is possible to have it too tight. When you ease the mainsheet, the boom should go away at about a 40-degree angle. Not straight out - up a bit!

FOOTING AND POINTING: THROUGH THE GEARS TO WINDWARD

If you overstand the windward mark pull on more vang, then keep sheeting the main to trim the boat.

To go high, perhaps because someone is close below you at the start, remember that the key is speed. Then feather up when the speed is high or when you get a favourable wave. Maybe loosen the vang a bit, to help pointing.

Footing.

Tacking in medium winds.

TACKING

You need not necessarily have the fastest or most extravagant tacking style but it needs to be consistent. If you can string together ten good tacks in a row or a good tack whenever you need it in whatever situation, then your tacking is good enough. For instance if you come off the pin end of the startline and can (marginally) tack and cross the fleet you need to have the belief that you can pull off a good tack. If you are at the stage where your first tack is brilliant and the next two are poor you will be taking a risk.

The most important thing is to tack in a flat spot. The Laser is a light boat so tacking in chop is really bad.

If you have to tack in waves, use them to your advantage. The technique is to begin your tack just before the wave so that as you sail into the wave it helps to push the bow up into the wind. Complete the turn through the wind at the top of the wave where the boat will have the least drag and waterline. Use the back of the wave to try and accelerate the boat out of the tack. Many people see taking in waves as a hindrance but if it is done properly it can actually make the tacks faster.

In medium winds the aim is to come out of the tack fast, rather than to try and make gains to windward.

If it is done properly the acceleration out of the tack should be quicker than the full upwind speed. Use an average amount of heel.

- Make a nice slow turn into the wind, with your body weight coming in at the same rate as the boat is rolling flat and over to windward. Increase the rate of turn as the boat comes head-to-wind.

- Take the boat 15 degrees further than close-hauled on the new tack, ease the main (about two feet between the blocks) and build speed. Change hands very quickly so you can sheet in hard, at the same time bouncing the boat flat and turning back towards the wind - all three together give good acceleration.

Tack like this in medium and strong winds. You should always be roll tacking to some extent.

Common mistakes

It's slow if you heel the boat to leeward as you begin the tack.

Some people sail for ages with the tiller behind their back, but I prefer to get my hands sorted out immediately and pump the sheet in.

Now view the Tacking video on the CD

Tacking in light winds.

Light winds

Roll tacking in light wind requires a lot of balance. It is important that only small and subtle rudder movements are made, while body movement and boat heel are used to turn the boat. Unlike the other tacking techniques the rate of turn needs to be adjusted. As you go into the tack turn the boat into the wind very slowly to gain as much distance into the wind as possible.

Once the boat starts to heel on top of you, increase the rate of turn by using slightly more rudder. As you come across the boat use the toestrap to pull yourself up to the new windward side. The boat should now be well-heeled so that the leeward deck is slightly submerged. As you bring the boat flat to accelerate make sure that the tiller is straight and that the mainsheet is eased a fair way otherwise the boat will just stall as you try to accelerate away.

Tacking in light winds - another perspective.

To sum up:

- Don't heel to leeward before you start.
- Begin to steer up and...
- pull in the mainsheet and...
- push away on the centreboard with your front foot.
- Once the boat gets head-to-wind the mainsheet hand goes onto the toestrap which helps pull you across the boat at the right time with the roll.
- As you get onto the new side the boat is well heeled and the mainsheet has been eased about two feet.
- Change hands straight away and sheet in again as the boat comes down flat.
- Take the front foot around the mainsheet again.
- Put the tiller behind you so you're set up on the new tack.

Now view the Roll Tacking video on the CD

Tacking in a breeze.

Tacking in strong winds

When tacking in breeze you need to be fast
into the tack and fast out of it. You also need
to turn the boat quickly through the tacking
angle and come away from the tack well
below close-hauled, because the boat will
slow very quickly once it starts going through
the wind. If you do a slow tack in these
conditions the boat will slow considerably
and in the worst case scenario get stuck in
irons or head-to-wind.

Even in strong winds it is important that you
roll the boat through the tack by staying on
the windward side until the boat is through
the eye of the wind. This saves on the amount
of rudder needed to turn the boat and also
means that the change from one side of the
boat to the other is one constant movement,
which is much slicker and more effective.

Gusty conditions

Balance and feel are crucial when tacking
in gusty conditions. Again it is better to tack
the boat quickly to reduce the chance of
a change in windspeed affecting the tack.
During the tack you will need to adjust your
movement across the boat in time with the
wind. If a gust comes on then get to the new
windward side quickly and vice-versa, to
keep the boat as steady as possible. Also
you may not need to turn the boat as far
through the wind; this is a mistake I used to
make especially in Sydney. If you know you
are tacking onto a lifting puff then effectively
you only need to steer half or three-quarters
of the angle that you would normally steer,
as the wind is shifting with you. If you steer
the full amount you end up coming out of the
tack far too deep, making leeway and with
too much power in the sail.

Rounding the windward mark.   *Turn tightly.*   *Sheet out.*
Mainsheet, vang, outhaul.

ROUNDING THE WINDWARD MARK

Sometimes, if you're struggling to make the mark, you can't adjust anything before you reach it. But if I'm laying it ok quite a lot happens before the buoy:

- I check the mainsheet is free to run.
- I let off as much vang as I can (the elastic holds it in).
- I luff so I can lean in and let off the outhaul.
- I turn quickly and use the turn to squirt the boat forwards.

At or after the buoy:

- Let out the mainsheet.
- Pull up the centreboard.
- Let off the cunningham and (if necessary) push up the luff of the sail.
- Let off the rest of the vang.
- Tighten the toestrap.

Now view the Windward Mark video on the CD

Centreboard.   Cunningham.   Vang.

REACHING IN MEDIUM WINDS

It took me many years to work out how to reach quickly. For a long time I thought I was quick enough but I hadn't realised what gains could be made. I trained with Mark Littlejohn for many years but was never able to go as fast as him on the reaches. It wasn't until Mark and I were training for the ISAF worlds in Dubai that I was finally able to learn from him how to reach quickly. The secrets are having plenty of vang

Vang settings: too loose.   *Correct.*   *Too tight.*

The tail of the vang is taken to the centreboard so you can grab it. You will constantly be adjusting the vang down the reach.

tension, being able to focus really hard on the waves and your speed, and sailing large angles with the wind and waves. I owe Mark a lot for his help over the years but it was my improvement on the reaching legs that was the biggest jump I have ever made and it made the biggest difference to my results on the racecourse.

Vang

The vang setting is vital to your speed while reaching. If the vang is set too loose the leech on the sail will fall off and you will lose too much power. If the vang if set too tight then the leech will hook too much, stalling the wind as it flows over the sail. While reaching if you can picture the sail like an aircraft wing it can be a good comparison. Putting too much vang on is similar to lowering the flaps on landing, it stalls the wind and is slow. Having too little vang is like taking away the area of the wing, you have less power. It is critical that you adjust the vang through the gusts and lulls to keep the correct sail shape.

Over time you'll get a good visual idea of how it works and you will naturally go to that. In a light spot keep heading up to keep the boat planing and let the boat heel. When a gust arrives bear away back to the proper course and pull her flat to squirt the boat away. Adjusting the heel also helps you steer without using the rudder! If you stop planing, getting it going again takes too much time so be prepared to sail big angles.

Use your body to push the boat forward when you feel it about to come off the plane.

Cunningham

As loose as possible

Outhaul

On a tiny bit so the sail is not too full. On a reach you're going quite fast so, like the wing of a jet plane, you don't want too big a chord.

Mainsheet

Take the sheet from the block, not the boom. This gives a better sheeting angle, and is better when you're using the tiller extension hand to help sheet quickly. Also it avoids that tangle you get at the bottom mark.

Set the outhaul like this.

Sit

I move my weight around quite a lot. Sometimes right forward when I'm coming down a wave to help push the boat. Sometimes I move my weight back to help the boat accelerate when the breeze comes on.

Toestrap

As tight as possible. It is faster as you are locked into the boat, your body movements are more effective and your backside won't drag in the water.

Centreboard

Only up about nine inches. You need lots of pressure on the foils to push against with your body weight and to resist the wind. If it's too far down you get too much drag. Too high and you're not getting the most power from the boat.

This is how far you need to move to keep the boat on the plane.

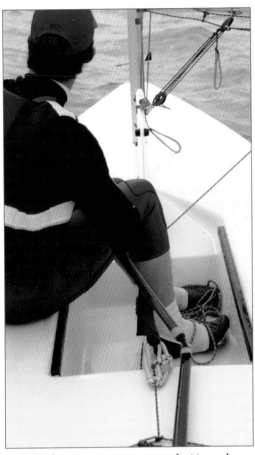

Sit in the boat so you can use your feet to push.

Common mistakes

Most people have the vang too tight or too loose and don't move their body weight enough. If the breeze dies they let the boat heel to windward which is really slow.

Keep the boat flat or slightly heeled so you've never got any lee helm on the rudder. Also, most sailors don't steer enough with the wind and the waves to keep the boat planing.

CD **Now view the Reaching video on the CD**

Reaching in light airs.

REACHING IN LIGHT AIRS

Cunningham

Off all the way

Vang

Tighter than you think. You want the leech to flick with waves and body movement, but not so loose that you lose power. A lot less than block-to-block.

Outhaul

Same as for the beat. In very light winds pull it on a bit.

Sit

As far forward as you can, 'on your toes' so you can move in and out easily. If the cockpit gets water in it, heel the boat and kick it out.

Sheet

Through the blocks, except in very light winds when I take it from the boom. Put the ratchet off.

Steer

Up in a lull, down in a puff to keep the speed going.

Centreboard

Quite well down, to give something to work against when you're rocking the boat. (Say 5 or 6 inches up.)

Common mistakes

Not moving body weight enough with different wind strengths.

Not heeling enough.

Vang too loose or too tight - all the leech telltales should be flying.

Sail in too tight - better to have it too loose. Watch the bottom telltale carefully.

In chop, let the boat heel then bring it back up to get the speed back on.

REACHING IN STRONG WINDS

To go fast be aggressive with your sail trim to keep the boat on the edge of all the power it can take, and balanced. Sail higher in the lulls to keep the speed on, then when a big gust hits ride that low with all the speed you can take.

Body position/movement/trim

In strong winds you need to get your body weight as far back as possible to keep the bow out of the water, while being able to trim the sail and hike hard to keep the boat flat. You will find that in large waves you need to move your body weight backwards and forwards to keep the boat's trim correct and help the boat surf down the waves. In strong winds set the toestrap really tight to help keep your legs locked onto the boat and also to keep your backside out of the water.

In strong winds it is hard to keep the boat level and steady. To counter this lots of mainsheet trimming is required to stop the boat from heeling too much or from coming over to windward. The correct heel angle is slightly to leeward - if the boat comes to windward then you will hit the water and have to use lee helm, both of which are very slow. A slight leeward heel gives you some flexibility and is far safer then trying to sail the boat flat.

The sheeting needs to be very rapid in order to keep the boat properly trimmed. Ease the sheet by letting it run through your hands and then suddenly jamming it off - this is similar to a pump and is a very fast way of losing power in the sail. In the lulls when you have less power in the rig you need to take all the height to windward so that when a big gust comes you can take the boat lower, with extra speed. If the wind is quite constant then the best course is straight to the next mark, sailing the fastest angles possible.

Toestrap

Tight

Cunningham

Normally your cunningham should be totally eased to give the sail the best shape and most power. However, if it is really windy and you are overpowered then pull on the cunningham. This will help de-power the rig and open the upper leech of the sail.

Vang

Quite tight but keep the leech partly open to get rid of some of the power. Adjust it after the windward mark when you're settled.

*A tight toestrap keeps your backside
out of the water.*

Centreboard

Quite well down. Any higher and the boat
gets too tippy.

Course

If it's a windy tight reach I normally go high
at first then low at the end. It's the best way
to overtake people, too.

Common mistakes

Dipping the boom in the water
- play the main more!

Vang too tight.

Not tightening the toestrap. If the toestrap
is not tight enough you will not be secure
in the boat. Your feet will be up in the air
and your backside in the water. Not fast!

Outhaul

In a fresh breeze (15 knots and over) the
outhaul should be left as it was for upwind.
When you let off the cunningham it has the
same effect as easing the outhaul slightly
and for this amount of breeze you are not
really looking for more power. If the breeze
is any lighter then the outhaul needs to be
eased before you round the weather mark
(it is very hard to do it on a reach or run).
Again you need to think of the sail as an
aircraft wing. If you ease the outhaul too
much the sail will be too full and stall.
If the outhaul is too tight then the sail will
not generate enough power.

Gybing in medium winds. Switch hands late, when you're steady.

GYBING IN MEDIUM WINDS

Gybing is all about turning the boat when it's going fastest and using a nice smooth roll to help the sail across.

It's vital to pick the right wave to gybe on. Sometimes, even though you're surfing, you don't want to gybe because you're coming to the end of the wave. The best time is as you catch a wave, or if you think you can catch the wave by roll gybing.

Pull in the sheet a bit before you start and use a lot of roll so you have really good speed as you come out of the gybe. As the strain comes off the mainsheet give it a short sharp jerk. Push the boom across with your hand to speed things up still further. Unless there's plenty of wind come out of the gybe quite high to help the boat accelerate: overall, turn smoothly

through a big angle.

In the middle of the gybe keep your body weight in the same position and the boat will roll over on top of you. Use your front hand on the toestrap to hang on. Sheet in a little bit more, and choose the right moment to cross the boat. As you go, push the boom across with that same front hand.

I wait quite a long time before I change hands to make sure that I'm steering in the right direction. Changing fast is not as important as it is after a tack.

One of the most common problems is getting the mainsheet caught round the stern of the boat. This happens when the boat is turned at slow speed with no heel and you forget to pull in the main. The sheet hits the water, gets dragged backwards and when the boom

comes across, the sheet catches the corner of the stern.

If the mainsheet does get caught don't panic. Try to keep the boat heading dead downwind before you move to the back of the boat and unhook the sheet. If you try to do this at any other angle there will be too much power in the rig and you will lose control.

Think ahead and set the controls for the new leg before you gybe. For example, if you are going from a run to a tight reach it will be hard to get the controls on after the gybe, so set them before you begin.

Push the boom across, mid-gybe.

Gybing - a bird's eye view.

ROLL GYBING IN LIGHT AIRS

Roll gybing in light airs is similar to tacking in light airs in that you use your body weight as much as the tiller to change course. Heel the boat windward to help it bear away. As you come almost square to the wind start sheeting in rapidly - once the boom starts coming across the boat use the toestrap to pull yourself to the new windward side. Be subtle with how much weight you use to bring the boat flat because you want the boat to flatten out nice and smoothly. As the sail fills on the new gybe hold the sheet tight to gain the most out of the roll and then ease to the normal setting. If you don't sheet the sail in for the gybe you will find that as you come out of it you will have no resistance to the roll and your acceleration will be poor.

GYBING IN STRONG WINDS

This is the same as for medium winds, except you don't need to roll as much to keep your speed on. Just make sure the boat's surfing flat out, to reduce the power in the rig. If you're worried about falling in (we all are) find the biggest wave you can to gybe on. Make sure the centreboard is up nine inches. This is the same for reaching and running, except maybe for light air running.

RUNNING IN MEDIUM WINDS

Sailing a Laser fast downwind is an art. There is no right or wrong way to sail downwind and many different techniques seem to be as fast as each other.

There is no doubt that being fast downwind is essential for any serious racer. Often people overlook the gains which can be made and they are often greater than the gains you can make upwind. I would largely attribute my success in Lasers to being one of the fastest downwind. So many times making large gains downwind has pulled me out of a mid-fleet position and back into contention with the leaders. It is the biggest 'get out of jail free card' you can have.

In the old days most people thought that the quickest way to the bottom mark was to sail the shortest distance, with the exception of finding the best breeze. Skiff sailors were the first to realise that going straight downwind wasn't necessarily the fastest route. In the early 90's the top Laser sailors, led by Robert Scheidt and his team mate Peter Transcheidt, started developing a new technique sailing large angles downwind in search of greater speed and the ability to catch waves. The changes in course then led to looser vang tensions to make the boat more versatile and help it to accelerate out of changes in course.

Sail angles to try to get enough power in the sail to catch waves. It's similar to changing gear in a car if you want to overtake. Once you've got the power in the sail it gives you the ability to then surf down a wave, when you find an appropriate one. In short, you're going off the straight line in order to speed up and then using that speed to go down a wave.

The biggest mistake everyone makes is picking the wrong wave to go for! If you go for a wave and don't catch it then you lose a lot of ground so be patient, wait for the right wave and take that. Also, realise you're not going to catch every wave but if you catch one wave really well it's five times better than catching half a wave.

Running in medium airs. Set the sail hike like this.

I'm not concerned how far off the rhumb line I go, within reason. I come up as far as I need, to get the power in the sail.

If you have headed up to get speed the only option you have is to bear away to ride the wave. Then the fastest option is to keep bearing away and end up running along the wave by the lee (rather than heading back up, which is a larger turn than simply continuing to bear away by the lee).

Work in your turns so you can go whichever way the wave is taking you. The more you turn the boat without using the rudder, the quicker it will be. Go with the flow! If the wave is trying to turn you right, go right. It's a bit like surfing - when you come to the end of the wave, cut back and take the next one. Although on a good wave you can go back-and-forth on it.

Cunningham

Right off.

Running on starboard. My left foot stops me falling backwards when I bear away. I can push with my left knee when I want to luff. I use my front foot to lift up my body and to move my weight forwards and backwards.

Vang

Loose! Pre-set it so the leech is nicely open most of the time. Too loose, and you lose too much power. The leech will constantly flick to squirt you forwards.

Outhaul

Loose - all the way off.

Mainsheet

Sailing by the lee, just past 90 degrees. Not too much, because with a loose leech the sail goes forward anyway. Sheet in quite a lot when you come up.

When making the turns, turn up at the right time, which is before you stop planing. Heeling the boat to leeward helps the turn. Turning the other way, roll the boat to windward to make it bear away.

Sit

I move my weight forwards and backwards but normally as far forwards as possible. Sometimes, when I'm trying to catch a wave my weight will be back, then I'll push it really far forwards to help push the boat down the wave. Use your feet to stay in! I sit sideways, one foot locked up against my side of the cockpit. The other knee or foot is pressed against the leeward side of the cockpit for balance in the waves.

Bearing away and heading up to stay on a wave.

Gusts and lulls

In the light spots you need to sail bigger angles to catch a wave and at some point you will realise you're not going to catch any waves, so start thinking about pointing back at the mark again.

Unless you can catch waves, there's no point in sailing extra distance.

The windier it gets the smaller the angles, because you have power in the sail anyway and you can ride the waves down to the buoy.

On form? Ask all the top sailors. Sometimes they can get in the groove and sometimes they just can't find it. If you're too tense, you must relax. Don't try too hard.

If you zoom down a wave and head for the one in front you can either try and sail through it and hop onto the next one, which is really quick, or bear away or head up, depending on where the buoy is.

Common mistakes

Steering too much.
Trying to catch waves which you're not going to catch.

Body weight too far back. You can never have the weight too far forwards until you're surfing, then move it back.

Now view the Running video on the CD

Running in light winds.

RUNNING IN LIGHT AIRS

The trick is to sail the angles, but this time it is to keep the speed rather than looking for waves. If you can get your speed up then this will produce more apparent wind which you will be able to use to sail the boat lower but with more wind. Lasers also go very well in light airs when sailed by the lee. Sailing by the lee has two main benefits: it helps to keep the boom from falling into the middle of the

boat in really light airs and it is also easier to tell if you are sailing a good angle to the wind. If you are sailing by the lee too much then you will find you need to use a lot of helm to keep the boat on a steady course and so the best course is just off the angle when the rudder loads up.

In lighter airs I change my seating position to facing forwards with my back leg and calf under the toestrap for support and balance.

sail and slow you down.

I developed a good technique in Sydney for really light air runs: I sat forward by the centreboard with my back leg in the cockpit and my forward leg stretched out against the vang. The forward leg holds the vang and stops the boom from coming into the middle of the boat when it loses the wind. It prevents all of those slow moments when you have to move forwards to push the boom out, which are effectively pushing the boat backwards.

Vang

To its loosest setting. Onshore, go to the clew and flick the sail either side and if the leech is just opening, that's the right vang setting. Adjust the rope at the bottom so this is the loosest setting.

When sailing return to this. The leech should just open if it gets some wind in it.

Centreboard

A bit higher.

Steer

Always try to sail by the lee and heel the boat to windward. As you feel the pressure coming on the sail counter it by bringing your body weight in slightly which helps push the boat forward.

Mainsheet

About 90 degrees, which is ideal. As the wind drops let it out further and sail more by the lee. Heel the boat to windward to reduce the wetted area, balance the helm and keep the sail out.

Sit

As far forward as possible. Front leg up against the centreboard and back leg wrapped under the toestrap for support.

This position makes It much easier to heel the boat over to weather which is fast because you reduce the wetted surface area of the hull in the water and so reduce drag. I also find that it is easier to trim the sail by taking the mainsheet straight from the boom rather than through the ratchet block. It reduces the friction and gives you a better feel for the wind in the sail. The key to light airs is to be as smooth as possible – any jerky movements will spill the wind out of the

Running in light winds.

Centreboard

The further you run by the lee, the further down the centreboard should be.

Toestrap

Tight.

Gusts and lulls

In a gust head more towards the mark.
In a lull sail by the lee to keep the speed on.
Look for the next gust coming down and sail over towards it.

Common mistakes

Boom too far forward.
You're just wasting ground.

Sailing straight to the mark. You'll gain if you run by the lee one way, gybe, and sail back by the lee the other way.

Sitting too far back.

You can adjust everything on the run

RUNNING IN STRONG WINDS

Set everything as for medium winds -
and go for it!

The main difference from medium winds is
you don't have to head up as much to get the
power in the sail, so you're not sailing such
big angles. If you catch a wave you can hold it
longer and sometimes you can jump a wave,
which is very fast.

You need an elastic loop to stop the vang
falling out of the boom.

Try not to get too far off course. The most I'd
ever do is three turns in one direction before
making the turn in the other direction - eg. three
lefts then right. Very roughly, you'll need to
make a turn every 10 seconds, so 30 seconds
in one direction.

If you find yourself rolling in to windward
push the tiller away, sheet in slightly and
(if you have all your weight on your legs)
move slowly into the cockpit. If the roll isn't
too dramatic you can sometimes use it to turn
away and sail by the lee.

Push the tiller away and sheet in slightly. Be careful not to pull your weight in too hard or you will push the weather deck down and swim.

In survival conditions

In conditions over 20 knots it is often a case of just hanging on. Your weight should be as far back in the cockpit as possible to prevent nose-diving. It is often easier to steer by holding onto the tiller extension close to the joint and it also gives you a better feel for the rudder. Lock your body into the boat by pressing your back knee up against the cockpit side with your front foot up against the front of the cockpit. The more secure you are the more control you will have. Around 20 knots you should still be working the boat to get the best out of it as there are still big gains to be made against people who are just sailing safely. Keep working the waves and the fastest angle to the wind.

As the breeze gets over 25 knots the fastest course is often straight to the mark as the boat will plane dead downwind. The safest course is either to sail slightly by the lee or on a broad reach, but then you are obviously sailing a greater distance. It is definitely a case of trial and error but the more you practise it the better you will be.

The leeward mark. Tighten outhaul, cunningham, vang, mainsheet, then fine tune after the mark.
Finally, slacken the toestrap.

APPROACHING THE LEEWARD MARK

All the sail controls are tightened just before the mark. First the outhaul, then the cunningham. Get as much vang on as you can, before going hell-for-leather on the mainsheet. The vang is then tightened a bit more after the mark and the other controls fine-tuned. Finally, slacken the toestrap.

Now view the Leeward Mark video on the CD

If you have to do a 720, first let off some vang. Then tack first (if you're beating, as here). Gybe first if you're running.

720 DEGREE TURNS

It is inevitable that at some stage you will need to make a 720 degree penalty turn. When sailing upwind start the turns by tacking and then bearing away. If you are sailing downwind then gybe first when starting the turns. This results in your coming out of the turns the quickest way and also on the same tack or gybe as you started.

In terms of boat set-up make sure your vang is well eased and that the centreboard is raised. If the vang is too tight you will not be able to bear away quickly. Having the board raised helps the swiftness of the tacks and gybes.

It is worth practising penalty turns even if you don't need to do many while racing. It is a good way of improving your boat handling skills!

CAPSIZING

Let's face it, we all capsize far more often than we would like to admit. If you are pushing the boat to the limit all of the way around the course then at some stage you'll lose control. There is capsizing and there is capsizing well. By capsizing well I mean in a way that you can recover quickly and reduce your loss. If you know the boat is going to capsize and is beyond recovery then let go of the tiller extension, as many sailors break their extensions in a capsize. Try to keep as close to the boat as possible and as soon as the mast has hit the water get onto the centreboard to stop the boat going all the way over. If you are unlucky and the boat has capsized into the wind then as you bring the boat up the sail will want to fill and push the boat the opposite way. If this happens you have two options: the San Francisco Roll (don't ask me why it's called that) or perching on the centreboard and jumping into the boat as it comes upright. The San Francisco Roll is a technique where you hold onto the centreboard and as the boat blows over you go under water still holding onto the centreboard and hopefully stopping the boat from capsizing again. I prefer to balance on the board and jump into the boat as it comes upright, it is much quicker but takes a bit of practice.

The most common capsize is the death roll to windward and half of the death rolls can be avoided. When the boat rolls over on top of you on the run you need to have a feel for how far you can go without capsizing. Many people bail out very early in a death roll as they think the boat is capsizing when in fact they could save the capsize if they had stayed in the boat. The trick is to steer hard to windward and sheet in hard. If the rudder had not stalled too much then the boat will stop bearing away, the wind will catch the sail and the boat should come upright. At least, that's the theory!

Part 3
Let's get personal

DIET

Being a Laser sailor is really no different from being a racing car driver. You need to be fit, healthy and the right weight to get the best out of your boat.

Training

While training your diet will depend on how hard you are training and what you are trying to do with your body weight, either to gain weight or lose it.

If you are trying to lose weight then you will need to cut out virtually all fat in your diet. Stay away from fast food restaurants (I know it's hard) and try to cook your own food as restaurant food is often higher in fat, that's why it tastes better. One very popular diet is to cut out carbohydrates and eat mainly proteins. This causes your body to burn more fat instead of carbohydrate. This diet can be very successful but it is important to remember that if you are training hard you will still need some carbohydrate for energy or you will get tired quickly and won't be able to train to your best ability.

Obviously, if you are trying to gain weight you will need to eat more. This is not an opportunity to buy shares in Buns R Us. You should be eating foods which are high in carbohydrate, along with vegetables and other foods which are high in protein. The trick is also not to put the weight on in fat but to build muscle which we know is heavier than fat and is of much more use while beating upwind in 30 knots. If you are struggling to eat enough try taking snacks in between meals, again not Mars bars but power bars or something which is a bit more nutritious. Vitamin and meal supplements are very popular for people who are trying to gain weight. I would agree that they can help but just make sure you are taking the right pills!!

Racing

In the week prior to the regatta you should be trying to build up your carbohydrate stores. You should by now have started tapering down your training programme and this will help you to store up more energy. Try to make sure the food you eat has some carbohydrate in it. The more carbohydrate you can store, the longer your energy reserves will last.

On a race day it would be nice to have a really big breakfast full of potatoes etc. but it's probably not a good idea as it takes time to settle and if you are nervous anyway, it won't help. Have a good nutritious breakfast instead. Also make sure you drink plenty as you can often be dehydrated in the mornings and this is the last thing you want to be when going afloat.

While you are out on the water it is important to have something to eat. Again you don't want to eat so much that it will make you feel uncomfortable but it is a good way to maintain your energy reserves. One of the most important times to have something to eat is after you have finished racing and are sailing back to the shore. If you eat within an hour of exercise your body will use the energy from the food in the most efficient way. Make sure you keep drinking to avoid dehydration. Some Laser sailors take a water bottle in their boat, either strapped to the mast or tied to the toestrap elastic. I have never done this but it can really help in very hot climates. There are many energy drinks on the market, I have tried most of them but in the end I just prefer water or a flavoured cordial.

In the evenings try to have a pasta or high carbohydrate meal which will help to top up your energy levels for the next day's racing.

The only real exception to this is if the winds have been and are likely to remain very light. If so maintaining this sort of diet may start increasing your body weight because the energy is not used up. If so, either do some light aerobic training to help burn up some energy or eat slightly less, especially in the evenings.

FITNESS

If there is one single aspect of Laser sailing which makes a difference it is fitness.

Fitness is so important. On a beat in windy conditions it comes down to the person who can put in the most effort who wins. I remember an epic race I once had with Robert Scheidt. It was the penultimate race of the 1997 Laser Worlds in Chile. Robert only had to finish around the top five to win while I was fighting it out for third place with Hamish Pepper. Anyway, by the last beat Robert and I were first and second with about two boat lengths separating us with the third boat out of contention. We ended up right out on the left hand layline with about ten minutes to go on port tack to the finish. It was absolutely neck and neck and I remember thinking 'I've got to win this one to salvage some pride'. Robert was really fired up to try and win both of the races that day and win in real style. As we came to the line there was about half a boat length in it as I just pipped Robert for the win. I will never forget that race, I think we were both pretty exhausted by that final beat although Robert probably had a lot of adrenalin running. I remember saying to myself 'well, you may have won the battle but he certainly won the war'. I realised that if I was going to win in the future then I needed to be able to race that hard in every race and it was then that the issue of fitness was really brought home to me.

There are essentially two types of fitness, sailing fitness and land fitness. Sailing fitness represents the state of sports specific muscles, the ones which are very hard to emulate in the gym or by other training apart from sailing. Land fitness is the general fitness training you perform away from the water, be it in the gym or out on a bike.

Sailing fitness

As I already mentioned, when you are out on the water you are using muscles which are very hard to simulate working in the gym. It is only by training on the water and working those muscles that your sailing fitness will improve

and you will be able to hike harder and for longer. Fitness training off the water does help but there is no real substitute for going out on a windy day and hiking till you drop. If you have to make a choice between fitness training on land or going out sailing in a breeze then sailing in a breeze is the way forward. It's a lot more fun as well.

Land training

Aerobic fitness

It does require very good aerobic fitness and stamina to be able to hike out and work the boat for long periods. You can achieve this a number of ways, running, cycling, swimming or even playing physical games like football. Cycling is probably the most sports specific as you are mostly using your leg muscles as you do when hiking. You are also less likely (as long as you don't fall off) to pick up an injury than when you are running or playing sports.

There are different types of aerobic training which you will need to use, depending on your base fitness and body weight. If you are around the correct weight then you should really work on improving your aerobic capacity. Again there are different methods of doing this but the one which I have used for the past five years is the OBLA session. Ideally you should see a sports scientist who will be able to work out your blood lactate level while exercising. From this it can be determined at what point of exersion your body begins to produce lactate, and this heart rate is your OBLA rate. It is normally two hundred minus your age. To complete the sessions you should then train at this heart rate for 25 - 30 minutes and complete about three sessions a week. It is hard work but is the quickest way to increase your aerobic capacity and keep you hiking out for longer.

If you are trying to reduce your weight then you will need to combine OBLA style training with long duration aerobic training. Exercising for long periods (1 - 2 hours at a low heart rate of 110 - 130) is the most effective way of losing body fat. If you do need to lose weight you should probably combine two or three of these long duration workouts with one or two of the OBLA sessions.

Weight training

It really depends on your weight and strength as to how much weight training you should do. You don't need to be Arnie to sail a Laser and if you feel strong enough in the boat then you should concentrate on aerobic training and more sports specific training. If you are desperately needing more weight and muscle then get some advice on setting up a good weight training programme. While it is important to work on hiking muscles be careful that you don't build an imbalance between muscle groups which might lead to injury in the future.

Sports specific exercises

Sit ups

Arm pulls

Back raises

Leg curls

Stretching

Travelling

If you are travelling from event to event it can be really hard to keep a good routine going. You don't need a gym to work-out – using your own body weight for sit-ups, pull-ups, push-ups and squats is better than nothing. It is important to keep a routine going otherwise you will loose motivation to keep up the training. The panels on pages 74-76 show what to do.

At a regatta

Try to get into a routine for each day's racing. It is a good idea to do some kind of aerobic training and stretching before you go on the water. In the evenings try to go for a light aerobic work-out and a long stretch, this really helps to stop your muscles aching if it has been a windy day.

HOW TO KEEP FIT IF YOU ARE AWAY FROM THE GYM

Running and cycling are always part of my training.

While training

I have always done my physical training after I have been sailing, following the principal that if you are tired before you go out on the water then you can't possibly sail to your best. I know there are other top sailors who do the opposite, so try both and see which suits you best.

If you are looking for more information on fitness for sailing and especially Laser sailing then excellent references are Michael Blackburn's book *Sail Fitter* and *Mental and Physical Fitness for Sailing* by John Derbyshire and Alan Beggs.

Push-ups.

Press-ups.

Pull-ups.

Sit-ups with twist. (Note you sit up forwards between each 'down'.)

Step-ups.

TRAINING

As I have already mentioned, time on the water is everything. Also, your time will be much better spent if you have an idea of what you want to achieve. Think what your weaknesses are in the given conditions. Also think about who you are training with, what you can learn from them and vice versa.

On your own

There will be times when you have no option but to train on your own. It is not as good as training with others but there are still plenty of areas you can work on and training exercises which can help you make the most of your time on the water.

Boat handling

Practise tacking. Your tacking can always be better and tacking practice also gives you a really good feel for the boat. If you want to push yourself harder tack every 30 seconds for five minute sequences. After five minutes take a break for a minute and then do another sequence and so on.

If there are any marker buoys around, practise holding the boat as close to the mark as possible. You can also simulate starting by giving yourself a 30 second countdown and then accelerate as fast as possible on the gun. Obviously it is a bit easier without any boats but you are using the same techniques which you will need in a real start.

Feel

While you are racing the more that you can keep your head out of the boat the better - it should be focussed on the wind coming down the course and the tactical aspects of the race - so long as you are not losing speed. To improve your feel for the boat sail along focused totally on what is happening to windward without turning your head back and try to see the wind coming towards you. The purpose of the exercise is that you improve your feel for the boat through the waves and wind so that you can sail it almost perfectly while focusing on

the racing. You need to repeat this exercise whenever you sail at a venue you are not familiar with; it should help you both find the right technique for the given conditions and get a better idea of the wind patterns over the course.

Something different

Training on your own also gives you the opportunity to try something a bit crazy and different like sitting backwards while sailing downwind. (Which will probably never work but at least you can have a go without embarrassing yourself in front of all the other sailors at your club.) It is while you are sailing on your own that you can also try little ideas which you have come up with and it may be that they make a real difference. You may not want to tell the whole world about this astonishing breakthrough in the art of righting a Laser as quick as possible, or whatever it may be but, if you have a training partner/partners you will be able to evaluate if it is really an improvement or just a whim.

It is always a laugh when you see a mate going on the water with some hair-brained way of tying their vang or cunningham or whatever, but it is really important that you are always thinking of ways to make the boat easier to sail or faster. Probably ninety percent of the ideas you come up with will be rubbish but is only by going through this process of trial and error that you find the ten percent breakthroughs.

Training partner

Sailing in Sydney was a real challenge. I knew I had to improve my performance in the shifty, gusty breeze and the flat water. I was very fortunate to have Paul Goodison as a training partner. Paul is a fantastic sailor in these conditions and this enabled me to try different techniques and boat set-up, knowing I could measure the results against someone who is one of the fastest. We would discuss our training sessions and try to analyse what had happened, why one person had a good day, or why not. The result was that I made a number of changes to my technique both downwind and upwind and also to my boat set-up especially in the way the toestrap was adjusted. I am sure that these changes made the difference; they certainly gave me a lot more confidence.

Ideally you should pair up with someone of a similar standard and who is able to put in as much time as yourself. It helps if you are a similar sort of age but what is most important is that you get on, can have a laugh together and share your thoughts on the day's sailing. When I first got into Lasers I teamed up with Mark Littlejohn. At that stage Mark was at the top of the fleet but needed someone to train with who wouldn't be an immediate threat. We were very close in light winds but as soon as the wind came up Mark was off in the distance somewhere and we soon realised that the better I could become in those conditions the more I would push Mark. In one winter we both improved dramatically in comparison to the rest of the fleet and after two years training together were first and third at the '96 Olympic trials. Mark then trained with me out in Savannah for the Olympics and coached me on and off up until the Olympics in Sydney. It is a good example in that we did not start at the same level, which would have made the first six months easier, but we both had the same goal and were prepared to work as hard as we could to get there.

Having somebody to train against gives you so many more options in terms of what to do on the water, someone to bounce ideas off and it also makes the time on the water a lot more enjoyable.

Coaching

Coaching can be a very easy way to bypass all the common mistakes, just as reading this book will hopefully guide you past some of the pitfalls that we make as Laser sailors. Ask around at your club or write to your Class Association to find out when and where there is coaching taking place. These sessions may not provide you with much one-on-one coaching but the training will be useful and you will also get a better idea of training exercises and may find someone who is keen to sail with you.

On an individual basis coaching can be extremely helpful especially if you are struggling with a certain technique or cannot find that extra bit to get you to the top. Often someone with a lot of experience who can watch from outside the boat or watch a race will be able to spot the mistakes or weaknesses and help get you back on track. If you can work with a coach over a period of time and have a good relationship then the coach will be able to sense how confident you are and to what level of your ability you are sailing, which makes life a lot easier. I worked with John Derbyshire for six years and in that time I learned to respect what he said and trust his opinions. John was also great at knowing what to say, and when. He would never try and make things sound better or worse than they really were, and that also gave me confidence.

It can, however, be all too easy to become reliant on a coach and so lose your own feeling and judgement for how you are sailing and how you can improve. I remember the great Russian sailor Valentin Mankin once telling me that 'a coach can only do so much, really good sailors should be able to coach themselves'.

Training methods

As soon as you have other boats then you can really take the training to another level.

Tuning

Line up about three boat lengths apart with the windward boat a boat length astern. Sail as hard as you can for as long as you feel is productive. As soon as one boat slips back, stop, talk about it and perhaps try a different setting for the next test. In stronger winds you can push yourself by doing five ten-minute sprints, sailing as hard as you can. This will really work the specific muscles and help to improve your sailing fitness. If you have more than five or six boats then it becomes really hard for boats to line up properly and stay in clear wind. Use a similar method for downwind tuning but for reaching it is probably better to start at intervals with the fastest starting last and trying to catch up. If you don't have any marks for the downwind tests then make sure you are all heading for a similar compass heading or point on the shore - it saves a lot of arguments.

Tacking

If you have a coach then line up as you would for a tuning run and get the coach to whistle every time he wants you to tack. Ideally you should start off slowly and by the end should be flat out. To put yourself under more pressure split into pairs with one boat behind the other and the boat behind trying to tack itself past the one in front, also good for a few arguments!!

Acceleration

Two - five boats line up head-to-wind as if on the startline with the most windward boat (i.e. starboard boat) counting down a one minute sequence. You are not allowed to sheet in before the gun goes but obviously the better you manoeuvre yourself the quicker you will accelerate compared with the other boats.

Rabbit starts

These are especially useful when you are without a coach and want a quick easy way to start a race. Ideally the rabbit should tack back within thirty seconds of the last boat crossing its stern. This can also be a good way to start a tuning run.

At a new venue you can use rabbit starts to help find out which side of the course is paying. Decide between you but make sure that you all have a different plan for the beat, be it to hit a corner or play the windshifts up the middle of the beat. Try doing a couple of these races to see if there is any correlation.

I can't emphasise enough that individually and as a group you need to have a plan for the training session and have talked about the areas you want to work on. Work on those areas you feel need most attention until you are confident you have made an improvement, then move on. Too many times I have gone out with a group and we haven't really discussed the training or what we want to achieve. You waste a lot of time and the whole focus of being on the water seems to disappear.

CLOTHING

It is so important to feel comfortable in the boat. If you are in any way restricted or feel too hot or cold it will affect your performance.

In hot climates stay cool. Lycra tops are a good way to keep the sun off. If the sun is very bright then you should wear a cap to protect your eyes. You may want to try sunglasses but if there is any spray the salt will dry on the lenses making it hard to see properly.

In the winter make sure you stay warm: if you get cold it's no fun and you are more likely to pull a muscle. Wear a woolly hat as you loose most of your heat through your head. Be careful not to wear so much that when you start racing you become too hot as this can also be really uncomfortable. At regattas it is a good idea to wear a coat out to the start. This will keep you warm while you are preparing for the start and you can pass it to a coach before the race.

Hiking shorts

For a Laser sailor hiking shorts are probably the most crucial item of clothing. There are many different makes but if you can find some which have stiff padding or battens then it will make your hiking much easier and more effective because they stop your blood from being cut off by the side of the boat. The Queensport pants are very popular but have a look at what is available and choose what suits you best.

If the conditions are very light you might want to wear some lighter hiking pants or just wetsuit shorts to save weight.

Boots

Boots are also very important. You need plenty of padding so that when you hike out your feet do not get bruised and sore. You also need to be able to feel the toestrap and feel steady on your feet while in the boat. I have tried many different makes of boot but always found that they slipped of my feet while I was hiking. In the end I selected a lightweight slipper with a grippe sole, like windsurfers use. Over the top of that I wear an ankle support, which you can buy from any sports shop. This gives you a good firm sole and plenty of padding against the toestrap as well as being lightweight.

Make sure your lifejacket does not sit too high on your shoulders as it is likely to catch on the boom.

Part 4
How to win
a championship

COUNTDOWN TO A PARTICULAR EVENT

Once you have decided which event is the most important to you, the one which you want to be at your peak performance for, you need to come up with a plan.

It goes something like this:

Logistics

- How long do you have until the event?
- How much time can you personally put in?
- How will you get to the event and how can you cover the finances?
- Where are you going to stay?
- Do you need to do any warm-up regattas?

In the perfect world you would spend as much time as possible training at the event venue. For my 2000 Olympic campaign I spent a total of nine and a half months over three years training on Sydney harbour. In reality most people cannot afford the time to do this so it is really a case of doing as much as you can when you can. It is also a good idea to chat to other sailors and find out what they are planning to do. If you are the only person training it can be a bit lonely after a couple of days, so try and get someone to train with.

To cut costs you could team up with some friends and travel together, which can also be a lot more fun. Similarly with accommodation it can be easier and cheaper to team up. If you are the sort of person who needs time to themselves then it might be better to sort out your own arrangements so you are able to get away if you feel the need.

You do not want to go for too long without any racing practice. Training is important but there is no substitute for the real thing especially if you are young and relatively inexperienced. So try to get to an event where you think the conditions might be similar to those which you are likely to encounter at the main event.

The venue

- What are the prevailing winds at that time of year?
- What is the climate at that time of year?
- Is the wind normally very shifty or steady?
- Is there much tide or current?
- Is it a nice place to spend some time?

You need to know what the conditions are like so that you can try and simulate your training to those conditions. You will have a better idea of which areas of your sailing you will need to work on improving. The wind strength will also have a big effect on your fitness training. If it is a light-wind venue then you might need to look at losing weight so that the boat is not too heavy. If the conditions are likely to be windy then you may need to do more weight training and eating in order to increase your strength and body weight.

The climate can have a big effect on your performance especially if you're not used to sailing in those conditions. If the temperature is very high you will need to look at what clothing you are going to wear and ways of keeping yourself hydrated.

If the winds and current are different from what you are used to then try to train where the conditions are similar. If you can't find anywhere then it will be more important to get to the venue early.

Make sure that you will be happy spending time at the venue and training there beforehand. If it is not your kind of place or for whatever reason you will not be happy there then minimise the amount of time you spend at the venue.

One good tip is to check with your National Authority. Other sailors or coaches may have raced or sailed at the venue. If you can talk to them or look at their notes it may give you a better idea of the conditions you will be up against

Weaknesses

Look hard at the areas where you feel you struggle while racing or training. The truth is sometimes hard to take but it is only by attacking them and overcoming them that you will be best prepared for the event.

Fitness

I have already talked about focusing your fitness routine around the conditions which are likely to be encountered. Other than that it is most important to be sailing fit and free of injury.

Peaking

All sailors' performances vary over time but it is crucial that when you hit the startline of the first race at this regatta that you are sailing to your maximum ability. If you train flat out for months and months you will turn up to the regatta tired and slightly unenthusiastic. You need to feel fresh and positive, ready to really go for it. For this reason it is important that you taper your training so that by the end you are only doing very short periods on the water and in the gym. That way your energy levels will increase and you will feel really fired up to get out there on the water and win. So make sure you plan your build-up to the regatta with this in mind.

RACING TO WIN

It is easy to make assumptions about winning but after much experience of racing Lasers the most successful are those who make the fewest mistakes, are able to pull something out of the bag when they need it and are the most consistent.

These days nearly all events are of twelve races or more, so this really puts the emphasis on consistency. Think of a series as a structure, you need some solid results in the early races to give you a good foundation to work from. As soon as you become inconsistent you are in trouble; it is the uncertainty which ruins your confidence leading to erratic decision-making and probably just as erratic results.

Psychology

I remember when I was in the Youth Squad, every year Jim Saltonstall would have evening lectures, which were great, but every now and then there would be a lecture on psychology. At the age of seventeen once psychology was mentioned I was off in a dream world and anyway 'I could just hike harder if I had a problem'.

I now know that psychology is the key to everything, in life and sport. What is going through your mind will affect how hard you train, how determined you are, your ability to deal with pressure, how you get on with your fellow competitors and your enjoyment of racing.

If you want to get to the top of the Laser fleet

then you have to be totally committed. The days of training at the weekend and summer holidays have gone. It has to be your job, hobby, life. I can say with some conviction that the reason people like Robert Scheidt and myself have been successful is that we put in more effort than most sailors. I remember one very good example of this was just before the '96 Olympics in Savannah. There was a warm-up regatta at Hilton Head, which is about 25 miles further down the coast. Robert and I sailed down there while the rest of the fleet either got their boats towed or driven to Hilton Head. We were lucky that it was a downwind sail on the way and when I sailed back it was also downwind but this meant very valuable time sailing in the strange and confused waves off Savannah and it paid off.

When you get out on the water you need to leave behind anything in your mind which is not connected to winning the race or sailing well. Forget about problems with your girlfriend, bank manager or whoever - your mind needs to be totally focused on the job in hand. Try not to get too involved with the social side - again it depends how serious you want to be but the more time spent chatting will drag your focus away from the racing.

You'll notice that the really top sailors are normally the most modest, the reason being that they know they are good so they don't need to tell everyone about it. If you hear someone blowing their own trumpet about a great start or something, just ignore it and go through your own mental de-brief of the race. This is really important as it enables you to pick out where you went wrong, areas you need to improve and the positives. You also don't get put off by the guy telling you that the only reason you pulled off that great port tack start was because he had to bear away for you and by the way you owe him a few beers. The more you go through the racing mentally the better prepared you will be for the next race. I really enjoy watching videos of sailing races, in any class of boat. Not only is it fun watching a good video but it is a form of mental rehearsal where you can also pick up tips from the racing.

At most regattas there are times when you will be held ashore due to a lack of or too much wind. All the hanging around can be really frustrating, boredom sets in and you lose all interest in going sailing or alternatively you get really wound up as you are dying to get out on the water and go racing. Try to have a plan for these situations which will give you something to do while not totally distracting you from getting ready to race. A bit of a kick around can be good fun (but make sure it doesn't get too aggressive), or try reading a book or playing a computer game.

When you hit the water you want to be ready. The very nature of the class means that the racing is very close and there are times when you will need to be very aggressive. You cannot afford to give an inch to anyone at any time. So be mentally prepared for some tough racing out there.

A TYPICAL RACE DAY

This is an example of a normal race day at a major regatta.

Wake up and go for a slow/ medium jog for 10 - 30 minutes with the emphasis being on stretching as much as possible to loosen you up for the day's racing.

Have a decent breakfast and read the paper or a book to help you relax. Pack your sailing kit and accessories. It might be useful to have a check list so that you don't forget anything vital, like your brain.

Try to arrive at the boat park about two hours before the start time of the first race. This will give you about an hour to sort out your boat before going afloat. Firstly turn your boat over and give it a wash and tip it up to check for water inside the hull (even if it was clean it is still reassuring to check). Rig up your boat making sure to double check fittings and ropes.

Once you are happy that the boat is all set go and check the noticeboard and try to get hold of the weather forecast. A decent weather forecast may help you decide on how to approach the day's racing and may answer questions like 'Do I need a raincoat to keep me warm between races?' 'Do I need heavy or light air hiking shorts, or both?' 'Should I have my light or heavy mainsheet?' The weather forecast will also help you to start running through the race strategy in your head. If you have a coach go through the forecast with them as they may have some good suggestions. Try to keep to yourself to give yourself time to think about the day's racing and check that both you and the boat are ready.

Unless the racecourse is either very far away or very close you should probably launch around an hour before the warning signal. There is always someone who wants to launch first and people who will give you a hard time for launching early but just stick to your routine. In '96 I was always one of the first to leave the shore at around an hour before the race. Then at the Olympics I was suddenly the last

to launch - it was really strange but showed how anxious we all were. I was happier sticking to my routine.

On the way out to the course try to get a feel for the wind and the waves. If it is a beat then sail close-hauled so that you can start to get in phase with the shifts. If the course is downwind and you are sailing near the position of the windward mark then stop and get a feel for how the wind is at the top of the course and take a wind bearing if you have a compass.

Once you are at the bottom of the course then sail an imaginary first beat at 80% effort so that you are sailing at proper angles to the wind while not exhausting yourself if it is windy. This should give you a better idea of the conditions, help you get in phase with the windshifts and pick up any current or tide out on the course area. Sailing properly upwind will also enable you to tune the boat and get an idea of what settings you will need for the race.

When you are happy with the conditions sail back down to the start and again make use of the time. Sail fast to get an idea of the techniques needed in the relevant conditions. Also try different gybes as you may find it faster on one gybe compared to the other. Try your absolute hardest not to capsize by pushing it too hard before the start as a wet sail and mast full of water is not at all fast.

Once the warning signal has gone then get your watch set for the preparatory signal.

After finishing the last race of the day try to sail or get towed in as quickly as possible, making sure you are warm enough and have something to eat to help re-build your energy levels.

Pack up the boat being sure to double-check all fittings and ropes. Then turn the boat over to check for any damage. If there are any problems fix them as soon as you are changed as it will never get done in the morning. If you have a protest then make sure you have the form ready to hand in well before the end of protest time.

Before you leave the boat park make sure you have checked the protest board (even if you were not involved in an incident someone might have made a mistake and involved you). Check to see if there are any changes to the sailing instructions and start times for the next day - almost everyone has been caught out by the start time for the next day being bought forward. Also check the results, even if you have had a terrible day it might get worse if your boat number was confused with another which was over the line in a race. It could also not be as bad as you feared. In the Danish Spring Cup in '99 there was one race where almost the whole fleet was over the line but the race was continued. I for one thought I had got away with it as I was well covered by other boats. We got ashore to find that the race officer had cunningly taken the numbers of the boats behind the line and disqualified the rest of the fleet, so you never know.

If it has been a really hard day physically I suggest going for a jog and then having a good stretch to help loosen stiff muscles. Otherwise don't party too hard, and get some decent sleep.

EXERCISING IN THE BOAT

It's good to stretch your legs on the way out to the course so you don't pull anything when you start racing, and you're nice and flexible for tacking and so on.

1. Stretch your quadriceps (which you'll use when you're hiking). These are the muscles which form the front of the thigh.

2. Stretch your back (to help with the twisting you do when you're working the boat upwind).

3. Stretch your hamstrings (which helps flexibility when you're tacking or gybing). These are the tendons at the back of the knee.

4. Stretch your calf muscles (which take a bit of a hammering when you're hiking). These are at the back of your leg, below the knee.

Stretching: Quadriceps.

Back.

Hamstrings.

Calves.

THE RACE

Pre-start

If you have a training partner then use each other before the start. At some stage you should split tacks, going for five minutes and then tacking back. This may help you to figure out which side of the course is favoured but make sure that the wind is not just oscillating, in which case both sides may be favoured.

It is good to have a routine for the pre-start so that you are not sailing around wondering what to do next. Before the warning signal goes you need to have passed any extra clothes and food to a coach boat. You also need to have come up with a plan for the race.

The plan should be based on the weather forecast, what you have learnt by sailing up the course both on previous days and on your earlier training run and the sailors you are racing against and trying to beat. If it is the last race of a regatta and there are only two of you in it you may want to stick with the competition rather than risk separating from them too much. Also if the conditions are those in which you know you are weak then you may need to try and push the start harder and also be more confident in splitting from the rest of the fleet.

Once the warning signal has gone you should be ready on your watch. Most events run the system 5, 4, 1 gun, so you should have no problem in getting the 4-minute gun.

You should now be trying to work out the line bias and there are a number of ways to do this. If you have a compass then use it to get a bearing of the startline and also the wind direction. If the wind direction is more than 90 degrees to the startline bearing then the starboard end of the line is favoured by however many degrees over 90 the difference is, and vice-versa. Eg. Wind 200, Startline 100. Square line = wind direction of 190^0. So the line is biased 10^0 to the starboard end. The easiest methods are either to sail head-to-wind on the startline and then judge which end of the line your bow is pointing towards, or sail

close-hauled away from both the starboard and port ends of the line and judge which end feels and looks better. Also bear in mind that what looks the favoured end of the line may not be. If for instance the wind is oscillating, in a couple of minutes you may have 10 - 20 degree windshift, or a rough sea may make one tack much quicker than the other and this will also affect which end of the line is favoured.

Your plan for the first beat may require you to start at the un-favoured end of the line but if you are really confident the side you want will pay then go for it (but you will need to make these decisions very quickly).

Try not to make your plan look too obvious, for example if you are planning to try and port tack the fleet don't sit by the pin end boat on port as the rest of the fleet will catch on and try to stop you. Leave your approach as late as possible.

Starting

Fleet sizes are normally large and so the start line is crowded. Lasers are relatively quick to accelerate so most boats are normally close to the line jostling for position very early in the starting sequence, unlike many other classes which tend to line up further back from the line to have plenty of time to accelerate. The rules allow you to move your tiller to steer the boat but you are not allowed to constantly move your tiller from side to side to propel the boat forwards. Therefore you need to work on a technique of using your tiller on one side of the boat's centreline and then after a while use the tiller on the opposite side of the boat to turn back. This should help to hold you in position without breaking the rules. You should try to have a good awareness for the positioning of the judge boats: if you know you are being watched then you may be doing something wrong, so be careful. Being able to handle the boat well in pre-start manoeuvring will only come with practice but this is something which you can do on your own.

The key to starting well in any boat is to be that split second ahead of the boats around you so that you are the first boat up to full speed and pop out ahead after the gun has gone. If you try to start ahead of the other boats around you then unless you are very sure of the where the line is you are vulnerable to starting early.

Accelerating off the line

To accelerate quickly you need to have at least a boat length of space to leeward to bear off into and gain speed. Don't go into a gap on the line too early and then start creating too much space to leeward as it will be too inviting for another boat to go in there and steal your spot. As soon as you feel it is time to go or the boats around you sheet in then you have got to go for it. Try to give the boat enough time to build speed before you head up to close hauled; this is why you need plenty of space to leeward. You really need to practise accelerating and in particular getting the mainsail in as quickly as possible. If it is windy then the vang tension is really crucial. If the vang is too tight you will find the boat very hard to manoeuvre and if too loose you will not have enough drive in the sail to help you accelerate.

The first 100 metres

As you come off the line try to keep as much speed as possible without being affected by the other boats. If you have a good start then try to punish those around you as much as possible by either sailing higher and so lee bowing those to weather or easing for speed and rolling over the top of the guys to leeward. Doing this will give you more options to tack or hold your lane. If you have a poor start then look to clear your air but don't be too hasty. Lasers are not as badly affected by sailing in dirty air as other boats. In fact if you can sail on the boat ahead's stern wake you can actually hold on to that boat. Wait for an opportune moment to tack away and then peel off. Don't give up, you still have plenty of opportunities to catch up.

While it is important to work the boat really hard off the line be conscious of the jury. It is at the start that the jury are most observant, so be careful.

Which way up the first beat?

If you can find some extra boatspeed off the start line and up the first beat then it will make life a lot easier. The saying that 'boatspeed makes you a tactical genius' is not far off the mark. As I said I have never used a compass as I find that using the angles of my competitors is just as good a guide to the wind and with the generally short courses which we now race on it is as much a percentage game as anything else. It is a case of getting in a good position and then trying to preserve that position by keeping between the majority of the fleet and the next mark. There will always be people who hit the corners and come screaming in with a great lead but if you can always sneak ahead of the main pack then you will be able to get to the windward mark in consistently

good shape. I'm not saying that if you really have a feeling that one side is going to pay you shouldn't go for it. If you feel you are losing ground on the boats around you then you are either not in phase with the windshifts or don't have the right boat set-up and are going slowly. You need to be able to realise quickly why you are losing ground and rectify the problem.

Windward mark

Most windward marks are hot spots for incidents and protests. There is also the prospect of gaining or losing large numbers of boats.

If you are in a good position at the front of the fleet then give yourself enough time to prepare for the bear away while not getting onto the starboard layline too early, because the further from the mark you are the harder it is to hit the layline smack on.

If you are struggling in mid-fleet then the approach to the windward mark is more interesting. If you are going to get on the starboard layline early then make sure you overstand slightly; if you don't then boats in front will tack on your wind and you'll find you have to keep tacking away for clear air. It can often pay to stay away from the starboard layline and all the bad air which comes from it and arrive at the mark on port. Remember that if you tack within two lengths of the mark you are very vulnerable under the rules. Also, approaching the windward mark on the port layline will cause you to have to sail through all the boats that are on the first reach or run, which is slow and hazardous. If you can try and predict what might happen as you approach the mark it will really help in your decision making, rather than screaming in and then suddenly realising you've got nowhere to go. If you see most of the fleet stacking up on the starboard layline then there is definitely the opportunity of gaining by not getting stuck in all that bad air too early. There are often big pile-ups at the windward mark as there are at the leeward marks.

My advice is that even if you are in the right it normally saves you a lot of time if you steer clear of trouble. The last thing you want is another boat sailing through your mainsheet and capsizing you. Again it is a case of thinking ahead and predicting where there may be trouble.

Reaching

I always used to think there was little chance of gaining much ground on the reaches but Mark Littlejohn taught me otherwise. If you have good speed then there are always opportunities to make big gains. When you begin the reach you have to assess the situation immediately. If you see the boats in front of you sail high then your likely gains will come from sailing low and vice-versa. It also helps to know your competitions strengths and weaknesses. If the sailor in front is the type who will never let you sail over the top of them, then you know you will have to try and draw them high of the rhumb line and then try to dive beneath them. Not only do you need to be fast but you need to be flexible in sailing large angles for a reaching leg. There will be times when you will have to sail far higher then the proper course to the next mark in order to get around a fleet of boats. It is the sailors who are able to sail fast at any angle and be aggressive enough to go for the overtaking manoeuvres who make the biggest gains.

There are a few definite rules for reaching. Firstly, on very tight reaches it hardly ever pays to sail low. The bad air of the surrounding boats is that much worse when sailing closer to the wind and you are also limited in your ability to accelerate as sailing any higher than the proper course will normally slow you down, especially in strong winds. The biggest gains are normally made by making an initial loss to get higher than the rest of the fleet and then trying to blast down over the top of the boats ahead; it's hard work but you can still make some good gains. Also try not to get forced into sailing high by the boats behind you. If you are confident in your speed then hold your course; unless the boats astern begin to affect your air you will end up gaining. If it is a reach to the finish line then you may have more options to sail low. Try to establish as early as possible which end of the finish line is favoured - the boats ahead may be a good reference for this. Too many sailors stop trying on this leg as they feel the race is already over, so here's your chance.

Running

Again, even before you get to the windward mark, try to establish which way you want to go down the run. This may also be determined by which way the boats in front are going. The most important factor is to be sailing in clear air. It is very hard to just sail through a group of boats, although it can be done. It is far easier to sail around the groups in clear air and clean waves. If you have a good lead or have few boats around you then your options are open: sail the quickest course possible. When a large group of boats is right behind snapping at your heels then you will have to take one side of the run or the other in order to keep clear air. There are also times when you are in mid-fleet that you come around the mark to find that the fleet has split to both sides of the run and in fact there is a clear lane straight down the middle. This can often be a great way to make huge gains. Like reaching, those who make the biggest gains are often the most extreme, eg. by sailing ridiculously large angles and extra distance in search of better wind and waves. The gains are often larger than those made on the upwind legs.

Leeward gates and gybe marks

As you approach the gybe mark consider whether you want to go high or low on the next reach. If the next leg is a run, then decide if you want to go left, right or down the middle. You will then need to set yourself up so that immediately after the gybe mark you are able to sail the course you want. Don't get caught out by other boats determining where you end up sailing.

The leeward gate is always quite an exiting part of the race. It is good to have a rough idea of which mark you are going to as you approach. This will be based upon which mark is closest to you, which way you want to go up the next beat and also which mark has fewer boats rounding it. However, you still need to be open minded as you approach the gate, watching the boats in front of you. A gap may appear where a boat in front peeled off for the other mark at the last minute.

If you are in mid-fleet the chances are that you will need to tack away after rounding to clear your air. In which case if you were wanting to head right up the beat then you may actually save two tacks by going around the right hand gate (as you look downwind).

Consolidation

Every point gained or lost is vital and you must fight for every place as in the end it will make the difference. At the Youth World Championships in 1994 Daniel Slater and I were very close on points throughout the regatta and the final race was desperately close. I won and Dan was 4th.The final result was that Dan won the championship. We had finished on equal points but Dan's discard was one place better than mine. Of course I was devastated at the time but it taught me an invaluable lesson. However badly you are doing in a race and whatever might have happened, whether it was your fault or not, you must never give up. In the end all of those places gained by giving everything until you have crossed the finish line will be the difference between being a winner or not. And I want you to be a winner.

The CD

The CD that accompanies this book shows nine key skills:

Starting	Windward Mark	Beating
Reaching	Tacking	Gybing
Roll Tacking	Running	Leeward Mark

INSTALLATION INSTRUCTIONS : WINDOWS

- Make sure you have Quicktime installed. If you do not, or you are unsure, there is a Quicktime installer on the CD in a folder called Quicktime Installer.
- Insert the CD. The program should start automatically in Windows XP and 2000 and in other versions of Windows (if you have Autorun enabled in the control panels).
- If the CD does not start automatically, you can start it by clicking on AINSLIE.EXE on the CD – it should now start.
- If the CD starts and you do not see any video. You will need to install the latest version of Quicktime either from the disc or from www.apple.com

Chose a topic, e.g. Starting. Click on **Starting** and the video will play, with pauses, to match Ben's voice.

To see the video at full speed, and/or another video, click the bar beneath the picture.

To stop the video and advance it frame-by-frame, click the buttons beneath the picture.

Each manoeuvre's key points are listed beneath the picture.

For more information, read the relevant chapter in this book.

MACINTOSH

Insert the CD. If it does not start automatically, double-click the Ainslie icon.
OSX users: This CD will run in classic mode only.

SYSTEM REQUIREMENTS

Windows.
Pentium P100 or better.
Windows NT, Windows 95, Windows 98, Windows 2000, ME, XP.
16-bit graphics card (millions of colours)
16-bit sound card.

MACINTOSH

PowerPC, System 7.6 or better.